Winter at a Summer House

Winter at a Summer House

Poems by

Mary Beth Hines

Cover art: Kerry Mullen
Author photo by David Mullen, of David Mullen Photography
(www.davidmullenphoto.com)

ISBN: 978-1-63980-045-2

Kelsay Books
502 South 1040 East, A-119
American Fork, Utah 84003
Kelsaybooks.com

For Steve—with all my love

And in memory of my parents, John and Mary (Murphy) Mullen

Acknowledgments

I am grateful to the following journals, which published many of these poems, sometimes in slightly different versions:

Amethyst Review: "May Procession"
Blue Unicorn: "Martha's Letter to Jesus," "Blue World"
Crab Orchard Review: "Destroying Angels"
Eclectica Magazine: "Working From Home During a Storm"
Gyroscope Review: "In a Cedar-Scented Drawer," "Marconi Beach"
Halfway Down the Stairs: "First Words"
Haunted Waters Press: "Alligator," "Winter at a Summer House" (reprint/*Mass Poetry*)
inScribe: Journal of Creative Writing: "Scarborough Sail" (reprint/ *The Orchards Poetry Journal*)
I-70 Review: "At Yeats's Grave"
Lighten Up Online: "Brightview on Blueberry Hill"
Literary Mama: "Heirloom," "Ritual"
Madcap Review: "Summer Messiah"
Mass Poetry-Poem of the Moment: "Winter at a Summer House"
MockingHeart Review: "Like Alice"
Muddy River Poetry Review: "Nauset Light Beach, November 2001," "Truth or Dare on the Bass River Bridge"
Naugatuck River Review: "On Bass River Road," "Joyride"
Nixes Mate Review: "Scargo Tower in December"
Panoply, A Literary Zine: "Bluegrass Baby"
Sky Island Journal: "Words"
Rat's Ass Review: "Cat and Mouse at the Broken Doll," The After Party," "Party at Collingwood," "Little Black Dress," "Water Running from the Hose," "You Win Some, You Lose Some," and "Sundown"
Rockvale Review: "Bath"
River Heron Review: "First Born"

Sparked by Joy: An Anthology of Contemporary Formal Poetry:
   "December," "Honeymoon"
Sparks of Calliope: "The Blue Chair Laments"
SWWIM Every Day: "Getting Ready for a Grandchild's Visit"
The Aurorean: "An Old Man Sings," "Ahab's Wife"
The Blue Nib: "October"
The Galway Review: "Providence," "An Old Man in His Chair,"
   "Year Round Beautiful," "A Child's Play," and "Swim Meet"
The Lake: "Salamander"
The Literary Nest: "Put Out the Light"
The Orchards Poetry Journal: "To the Red Maple in Spring,"
   "The Hand-Me-Down Jolly Jumper," "Scarborough Sail"
The Road Not Taken: A Journal of Formal Poetry: "Dunmanway,
   1914," "A Cry So Close To Song," "Before the Blizzard"
Thimble Literary Magazine: "The Wedding Dance"
Wickford Art Association: 2018 Poetry & Art Exhibit Anthology:
   "We"

I want to thank my husband Steve, who conceived of and set up, the beautiful space where I wrote most of these poems; who patiently endures my distracted mental state when writing; and shares with me all of the greatest ups and downs life bestows.

I am also immensely grateful to my sister, Kerry Mullen, for the book's cover art; to my brother, David Mullen, for my author's photo; and to my children, grandchildren, parents, and other dear family members and friends who inspired and encouraged me in the writing of these poems.

I thank the Lexington Community Education Program, the Farm Pond Writers Collective (generously hosted for years by my friend, Elizabeth Sheehan, Co-Founder of Care to Communities), the Cambridge Center for Adult Education, and the MIT Poetry Group (hosted for many years by the late Tunney Lee) where the earliest versions of many of these poems were conceived, shared and honed. I am particularly grateful to the respective leaders of the workshops in these programs—Tom Daley, Kelly Dumar, and Katia Kapovich. Your skill and attention made so many of these poems better. Your love of literature and dedication to teaching is inspiring. I appreciate your mentorship more than I can say.

I am also grateful to Alec Solomita for his careful reading and editing of the manuscript; to Deborah Marshall for her continual interest in and inspiration for my writing through the generous sharing of her own creative pursuits; to Rea Cassidy for her 40+ years of encouragement and cheerleading; and to my many amazing workshop colleagues who, over the years, have inspired, read, heard, and thoughtfully critiqued many of the poems in this collection: Kirk Abrams, Emily Axelrod, Wandajune Bishop-Towle, Margaret Bryant, Robert Carr, Camila Chaves, David Donna, Claudia Duchene, Karen Edwards, Judson Evans, Peggy Gavin, Ann Marie Glenn, Ric Haynes, Kate Hughes, Sue Kennedy, Leeanne Labelle, Evelyn Luchs, Kenric Nelson, Caitlin O'Halloran, Richard Perse, Phyllis Rittner, Liz Sheehan, Karin Stanley, Jill Smith, Gale Moran Slater, MJ Turner, and Megan Walls.

Contents

Six

One

First Born

He breathes blue
water for air,
dark whorl
of muscle, hair,
sea whistle
sways in wave
after wave
of shore
side light,
star pearl
spine, and heart
trilling blood
to burst
in the full
measure
of mother-strung
madness, chord
laid layer
upon layer,
until the sea
shell's music,
pillowed chime,
and he
once touched
tender and bagged
for safe
keeping, tips
and drops
in wail
amidst all
the blazing
wildness
of the tide-
thrashed world.

A Cry So Close To Song

That middle-of-the-night cry tears right through
my weeping, mounded flesh stretched full
of fresh, Grade A, mother's milk, the real
deal, pulsing and puddling. Who would have guessed
I'd fall in line at twenty-nine? As if on cue
my body grew a body through a wild
seed dropped onto my lawn—blossoming black
cherry tree fathered by a migratory bird.
And my child screams like a gull, all guzzle
and swallow, suck and squirm, scrabbles till he hollows
my insides out, cracks nipples black and blue.
But afterwards he curls in, silk-skinned, sated,
a milky-mouthed songbird, nestling, sedated.

Bath

Slipped from her onesie, tender-skinned, sleepy,
too small for her long name, but I never cared for *Lizzie.*

Young cousins, years back, used to call me Mary Bath—
at first sweetly guileless, later tinged with malice.

Still, I rather liked *bath* so bestowed *beth* on *Eliza,*
name with breath-soft suffix akin to *birth* and *death.*

Spare syllable to savor like salt and hot, mud and sun,
bird and ice, cat and blood and drown and tub.

As water rushes from the tap, rainbow bubbles
build then snap. Waves ripple her legs and chest.

Fingers prune. Limbs flail, starfish, stiffen.
Tongue in root, she wails a wake-up.

Newborn skin surprises palms. Her buttoned belly,
breath-fed, rises. Eggshell eyes glint baby-blind.

When the steam clears, back to simple—flutter kick
through cocoon swaddle—bath, moon, milk, mother.

The Hand-Me-Down Jolly Jumper

Of my five lives
I find this one finest.

This child knows how to ride.
They call him Baby Dino.

He screeches when he flies—
a mini pterodactyl.

When his feet slam the floor,
he springs and squeals for more.

I share his raucous glee,
and grieve to feel him growing,

hold on to his fat thighs,
beg him to never leave me.

December Song

We slip from the forest on charmed, slender legs.
Our eyes spark with starlight, we dip our sleek heads
toward the boy at the window reciting his prayers.
We're a dozen this evening—does, fawns, and a buck,
streaming through twilight to lure the small son
of the camouflaged hunter, to daze him with musk,
to enchant him with emerald moss, ice, owl song,
before he grows hungry, and skilled with a crossbow.
But the boy's still a baby, no need for our tricks.
He sees us in moonlight. We're gifts for a prince.
He steps out to greet us through snow cover, mist.
We kneel. He climbs on, nestles in for a ride,
while above Venus shines, and the Geminids fire.

Words

We speak the truth
with silence, he and I—
wizened warblers, our throats
trembling stillness in rise.

He, an infant, rooting
for first words—*Mama, Papa,*
me leaving behind years
of rushing words—

syncopated verbs, precise
diction, crosswords,
speeches, puns, pitches—
a labyrinth of language.

Though some chance refrains
still linger on my lips
along with the taste
of that last persimmon,

so heady and rich,
pulpy nectar, sipped
and savored down
to the last knife seed as

the baby cried
his distress disguised
as hunger for the tender
tongue of touch.

October

Papery orange
Chinese lanterns blossom—blaze
above cracked asphalt,

silver-flecked charcoal
tar spread as far as we two
can see from Goose Hill.

Baby's finger points—
please, to touch, sniff, tongue tender
jack-o'-lantern skin.

I brush a veined leaf,
seize and squeeze a stem—a head
lopped off. The child squeals.

Hush, I scold, peeling
back four clasped leaves to reveal
the poison berry.

First Words

ma as in mama as in grandmas as in aunties
ma as in milk as in moon   hip   lap   swing

ight as in light as in sun as in let there be
sparkle as in off as in on   look-look   see

da as in father as in man as in bearded one
pick me up   shoulder ride   squeeze my feet   sky

owey as in odie as in teeth as in tongue
owey as in breath as in wolf   pup   bark   romp

ayaya as in Alexa   play Baby Shark
Five Little Monkeys   dance party   stomp

uh-oh as in oops as in mess as in hahaha
uh-oh as in game as in play as in please don't stop

mine as in mine as in mine as in mine
as in hungry as in ma as in da as in want

The Wedding Dance

Nana hangs the gold-leaf frame in her kitchen.
Lifts me up, and hips me in to see it.

What strikes first is reeling, kissing, red—
then the bulging bagpipes and a flute.

Hats are helmets—black, brown, mostly white,
atop pale faces—gossips, lovers, watchers.

Big trees rise and loom over tripping clogs.
Scarlet scarves and skirts wing, skip, and swirl.

Nana points—*see there*—to a moony child
about to be knocked over by a giant.

I gasp. Glop spills in curdles from a jug.
I feel a crone's firm arm steady at my back.

I squint and lean in closer. Where's the bride?
Nana's fingers brush a lady in black.

She's fat and smiling, waltzing with her father.
Curly hair springs out from her rose crown.

I fuss to hear the music—*play it, play it.*
But Nana presses *hush,* fingers to my lips.

Silence creeps like her bittersweet between us,
pricking at my belly, redding her wet eyes.

I squeal when suddenly she bursts into singing.
Cheek-to-Cheek—she says—*an old wedding song.*

Then she tips me upside down and spins me,
and I spring wings so she'll never have to stop.

Two

Scarborough Sail

Father is a tall ship, holds me
steady in his square-rigged
sails above the roiling sea
before he tips to dip
my quaking shins, my knees
a little bit deeper
with each yelp and *please,*
please plea to lift
me higher, to pitch me
into the fray.

I holler and squeal,
keel head over heels
before I crash, scrabble, rally
and rise—taller, brighter,
keener with every try
until I'm clambering over
his creaky shoulders to leap
through quickening sky
into whitecaps, foam splash,
a madcap bowsprit ride.

I gasp when I swallow
a blast of salty water,
thrash a choppy freestyle,
spill into rip tide, swivel,
plunge, grapple until ropy
fingers net me, set me
face-to-breaker where I dive
the way he taught me,
beeline into surf swell,
under mayhem, into sparkle.

Ritual

Sunday afternoon and my turn
to kneel on the creaky yellow
kitchen step stool and bow
over the sink, unspool my locks
into the clean pool, the white
enamel basin. Two rust eyes blink
from the bottom. I bend my neck
for Mother's blessing. I might be clay.
I might be dough. Her pulsing
soap-slicked fingers sink and knead.

Faith

Up strides my five-year-old brother; behind him
two-year-old me. I clamber up, sit to pert
attention on the bearded stranger's knee.
Eyes locked on, we three gawk in quiet want
amidst jangle, babble, prattle, *Joy to the World.*

We might be magi. We might be cherubim,
David and I—the way we still, the way
we watch. The man's eyes blaze promises.
And we believe—all wide-eyed, tongue-tied desire.

And he—the man in the fur-trimmed suit
with his bushy brows, the blowzy nose—
he might be a 1960's Jesus framed
as he is on his tasseled throne
against the photographer's fraying backdrop.

No words for this, my brother and I purse
our lips, sniff to dizzy the sugared fumes wafting
from the in-store oven—Jordan Marsh's blueberry
muffins—and the minty sparkle of the old
man's breath—ever-after rose, frankincense, myrrh.

May Procession

We sail on lace
feathered arms
into the glare of May
sunlight, shattering
the air with a chorus
of our nuns' saintly,
sweeping names.
They brush us into line.

We descend the grand
slope of cathedral stairs
sparkling with the ice
melt of a nearly
forgotten winter, and fly
to the hill over the river
where we hover
above the blare
of the sin-filled world.

A May Procession,
all blossom and yellow-
beaked, orange-tinged, pure
black and white, burning
hawthorn, and all of us
bloom and sway
and tip toward a fall
from the slick
bank into the whirling
water below.

A Child's Play

Dawn, and the child creeps down the stairs
simmering stealth, jet eyes, hinged limbs.
She drags, clambers up a creaky chair,
dips ten fingers into Bridie's
cage, old glass tank, fishes out the hair-
less pups, three to a palm, air-lifts
them from the gerbilarium.

Her magic-carpet hands dizzy
in rise, sweep and plunge, circle, whirl
a ricochet, guileless banshee,
she tips the newborns to the floor,
flicks them, whorled marbles, pale, moony.

On Bass River Road

Two small boys seesaw in their yard
after dark. Almost the same size,
perfect partners for the ride—
as one pushes off and flies up,
the other plummets, knuckles
bared to the bar.

Inside, their mother puts down her book
and tumbler of gin to listen
to the rise and fall of their voices
amidst the hum of crickets, the river
running just beyond their border.
Through the screen she teases out Cassiopeia,
the Milky Way running through her.

Hours later she startles awake and weaves
from window to door to yard. Her voice
shatters the silence with the boys' names.
She crashes through brush to the water's
edge, scans the dark river on her knees.

Back at the house the boys are asleep—
curled on an old mattress hidden
beneath the eaves in a dusty crawlspace
where the two of them fit
together, perfectly.

Put Out the Light

Put out the light and then *put out the light*
again. Long day done, Mom and Pop tuck
us in, clink glasses, turn the Coltrane up.
The saxophone sways, pivots, erupts.

I climb under sister Maisie's covers
where goose down muffles, and I can barely hear
the stutter of their feet, the bump and jeer
when one missteps and the other one stumbles.

Maisie's older so she knows what's what.
Tells me not to worry. Says it's how they love.
Sometimes grownups kiss. Sometimes they cut.
It's hard to explain but some like to draw blood.

Put out the light and then *put out the light.* Crack.
Bang. Maisie hugs me. We sleep tummy to back.

Like Alice

Secrets fang beneath smiles,
whispering crystalline shards,
and I, a child, caught off guard,
perch on kaleidoscope's bright
edge, swallowing the dizzy

whirl and fall into splays
of red and purple, sprawl
of cracks on a frozen pond
where I spin on skates, flung
from a steady, gloved hand

through sun-beamed air
and crash through land that silvers,
rusts, while I careen like white
water, punching and spilling end-
over-end through the earth's pale blue crust.

At Church in Quebec

Kneeling next to Mother on the Holy Stairs,
I gaze at the crutches left by the cured and scan
each riser to find the sacred relic embedded there.

I don't know any souls in Purgatory
so pray mainly for myself.

At the top, poised to race out, I stop when I see a tear,
and she looks for a moment like my grandmother—
small, soft-skinned and powdery.

I put an arm around her waist, grasp an elbow,
and pull her to her feet where she sways.

For the first time, I notice how her fingers tremble,
and I want to slip back inside, to murmur
more urgent prayers. But I slow, let her lean.

We lock arms and walk back to the car
parked so far away, where Father smokes cigarette-
after-cigarette and keeps an eye on the younger kids.

Salamander

At the bus stop drenched
in cold April rain Mother
unfurls her yellow
umbrella, a swaying
canopy of goldenrod
and bluebells, and invites
a dripping girl to join us
as we wait for the 505 bus
to sweep us from the curb
into the cool dark, to hurl
us into the story spilling
like confession from the woman
who in the half-light looks
like a young Dorothy Day
and Mother cannot
turn away even though
she wants to
cover her eyes
instead she slips off
her coat, drapes the girl,
bares her own thin skin
to soak in, exhale, the wrenching
bus air like the long-
tailed salamander I saw
through glass at the zoo years back—
its wet eyes, the spotted
full-body freeze
when I caught it
beneath the dome
of my fluorescent
hazel gaze.

Heirloom

Mother razes and wipes, razes and wipes
while the old oak groans beneath her fingers,

lodging a thin splinter into her palm when,
ungloved, she smooths a cross-grained edge.

She dresses the rough-hewn surface with spirits,
finishes sanding—gentler when the heavy work is done.

I sidle in then, surprise us both
by offering to help.

Together, we wipe the antique chest clean of dust,
kneel, and knead in stain with long strokes.

The wood darkens and ripples with coiling
tracks and lines as we brush on the last clear coat.

The heirloom shines in the cluttered garage,
ready for Mother's children to fill it, empty it.

We draw ourselves up to our feet, Mother's
mottled hands pressed to the small of her back,

aching for a few moments at the looming cleanup,
swaying in fumes. I decide then I'll catch her if she falls.

Three

Joyride

On a joyride through my old hometown to kill
some time, I pass an abandoned summer camp,
site of my first job—a lifeguard. I was one of a gaggle
of electric orange-suited girls slathered in baby oil
who patrolled a pool that sparkled with water bluer,
and clearer than any I'd seen before or have since.

The meadow next to the pool still bursts with sweetfern,
and when I stop the car, step out some forty years later,
a few leaves crushed underfoot resurrect the heat,
the slow afternoons, the god-like man we all wanted then.

We dubbed him Adonis the first time we saw him
striding across the grassy field. He was bearishly tall,
wore low-slung shorts. Muscles quivered beneath
taut skin. Tiny bright hairs licked calves to thighs.

I burned to win—juiced my hair, took up smoking,
crashed his raucous July Fourth party, scored a spin
on his red Ducati. I was wild with love but dared
not show it—to enthrall such a man meant rousing a chase.

He followed me one night down to the river, fingered
my wrist, lipped an ear. I pulled away, slipped out of my clothes,
leapt from the rope swing into the water—higher, smaller
till I disappeared. By August I was the straight up winner.

Now I lean on the car as the wind kicks up
that summer's fragrance—cut hay, remembered bodies,
campfire smoke winding backward through trees.
Bygone spirits arch in shadow, cross years, rush
and recede, still breathing through skin in air, in water.

Truth or Dare on the Bass River Bridge

Grace chooses the dare—
shuts her eyes and leaps
from the bridge.

Arms wide, she bows
and spins through the air.
Her red heart skips
and drops.

Above, the boys whistle
and roar. Grace surfaces
to see them plummet
one-by-one.

Then she turns and dives
deep into the river where
the watery landscape undulates
and she slides behind a wall
of swaying weeds and waits
for a handsome,
unsuspecting admirer.

Swim Meet

Lined up in our red
lycra suits, goggles taut
across skulls and tight
rubber caps, we shiver
in bodies shaved
smooth—even a hundredth
of a second matters.

Coach paces. Warm up
time is sacred and our star
breaststroker's late.
She's heaving in a stall—
hates to race the Boxers,
and today she must break
a minute twenty-eight
to make States.

The rest of us have learned
from our unsuccess
to savor the occasional first,
the burn off the blocks,
bodies cutting crimson
streaks through blue, the kick-
stroke-surge through the wake
of the winner's churn.

You Win Some, You Lose Some

You win some, you lose some, Fitzwilliam
grins, and his gold tooth glints.
Off with my shawl, my boots, a ring.

Lee's basement's freezing as I strip
off my layers, bet high and early,
bluff through my blue lips.

You can't lose 'em all, Lee was fond
of saying, back when she first
talked me into playing.

Round by round I grow closer
to a win despite a few tough losses
that demonstrate my grit.

Vince has great instincts,
Fitzy's proved a pro, and Lee,
ever-cautious, knows when to quit.

Two pairs beats one, and a straight
beats them both, and my clothes
in that pile means the game's finally over.

Seems you can't win for losing, Fitz
commiserates, as he stretches out his arms
to sweep his winnings in.

First Love

I chose you
all onyx shine
and glittering
silver keys, secret
hollows, flared
bell mouth, you,
my girlhood
B-flat clarinet,
nickel-plated
ligature, sweet
reeds splintering
my aspirational
embouchure,
so many
extravagant words
to curl my moody
tongue around.
My very first
infatuation lingered
an entire decade—
scales, études,
fantasias, and
Mr. Maier's weekly
lessons that went
beyond arpeggios
to breath control,
improvisation, trill
keys, espressivo.
We lasted through
the seventies, climaxing
with that Helliwell solo
on Breakfast in America,
afterwards nowhere
meaningful left to go.

Summer Messiah

Woodpeckers riot
outside Josie's window
early on Sunday morning.

A mountain of pillows on her head,
she smothers them drum-by-drum
but they bang on, amp up the joy.

She groans and rolls, knees to chest,
feet bloody from dancing barefoot
with the boys on Bolton Road.

When a hermit thrush hijacks
the chorus outside, Josie flushes
with dawning relief.

Recalls how she shook
last night's suitors, slipped
out a window, home.

Her bed sways in the thrush's chant—
    Oh holy holy holy
    Ah purity purity
    Eeh sweetly sweetly

She licks her lips and adds a joyous
voice to the din—pitch-perfect
for a Saturday night spinning into Sunday.

Party at Collingwood

Delicious Aloysius crashed our party last night.
He slipped in and clipped a beer and Maggie swore and roared
when she realized he'd entered but brought nothing in to share
except for his good looks and charm—enough for most of us—

but Maggie, as a feminist, demanded a lot more.
So shirtless Alex bounded up and danced the table tops
while Maggie in her hot pink dress woo-hooed and sang along
till Barney grabbed her by the waist and sailed around the room.

And Maggie's red hair flew and spun—sparked the party's fire,
although this morning nothing's left but pools of lost desire,
and Aloysius asleep, sprawled bare-assed across the floor,
next to Maggie, next to Barney, snoring like a wild boar.

Blue

I am the blonde with the blue
wings swinging between the framed
edges of my yearbook photo

loco, the boys in my class tease, my hair
a billowing affair following
my beauty day at the mall

all ready for the mob at the Sheraton
beyond prom where we girls fall
between squalls of boyish men

muddled and mauled we call for more
menthols, mercy, mudslides, more
mix to fix the spinning

stars to the ceiling for another
hour more, a moment to make
a wish, a trick of light, the door

swings open to *we are not
whores* our voices scratched with sore,
all those scores kept and secrets

mourned for years I felt
no pain and nearly married
the boy I cried about most days

and nights back then when
I found someone to bury my blue-
tinted head in someone who

forevered me on his back in burning
black, my tiny skull inked between
his blades spiraling blue-tipped flame.

Bluegrass Baby

I questioned love, twenty-one,
lost in the swelter of a Saint Louis
summer, seeking cool
in Soulard bars where a rave-eyed
music man stoked guitar.

My downfall: his Mississippi
riverboat calluses and all, fingered
chords, working man's hands
picked a pattern, conjured shimmer
from my dreadnought body.

Right out of the box he played me
throat to saddle, fretted my neck, bone
on brass strings, abalone, rosewood,
raised my pitch before he palmed
me mute with his strumming hand.

Blue World

This is so easy to begin.
You are strong and I am supple.
You are bone and I am marrow.
You are war and I am soldier.
Camouflage and platinum blonde.
You're top brass. I'm keen to follow.

We're a pair, or seem to be,
Through catastrophe and peace.
Before I'm krill and you're the whale,
I'm sparkle fish, you're ribbon eel.
We swim beneath a fickle sun
That fires the jealousies in us.

I am naïve you say I know
I am all heart too hard to love,
Fanatical, a Joan of Arc,
Narrow believer, easy mark,
That people should be as they seem
In pitch of night, in glare of morning.

You tell me that you're what you are.
I'm not to worry. I must trust.
Your whims for others sweep and fall.
Your need for me is mine-deep, solid.
You are wind and I'm sapphire.
I blue the world you whirl with fire.

Four

The After Party

We sweep into the clearing in prom gowns
and heels, pull silver flasks from purses, light
cigarettes. The air is alive with owls
and starlings, and we build a white
towering fire. We shimmer in its heat,
slip from tight dresses, weave hair with flowers.
Drunk on wine, we chant and drum, lurch to our feet
when we hear the boys' voices far-off
growing nearer—a brash, slurring babel.
Reeling shadows, hurtling music nearly smothers
our party. But we rebound and rattle
our black pine sabers, and chase faceless brothers,
strange suitors, lovers, until dawn when we stagger
home half-dressed, mute, blear-eyed to our mothers.

Dunmanway, 1914

Friday morning, light snow on Coole Mountain
changed to drizzle then biting sleet
as the girl trudged to school, past cows, townsmen,

the royal constabulary on Castle Street,
patrolling the square in their army green,
wool caps on heads, new boots on feet.

Their moon mottled faces, shaven clean,
loomed on necks snapped into uniforms.
Eyes down, she passed by, small, unseen,

remembering one boy from a year before.
Dark-haired, lithe, he hauled turf with her brothers
by day, by night teased kisses from her

on Pipe Hill behind tall, sprawling rushes.
But yesterday afternoon, in heaving
rain, he stalked into her school along with the others.

The class was quick though, prepared for deceiving.
Miss Walsh heard the gang coming two minutes out,
and the kids jammed the Irish they'd been reading

under floorboards, then watched the cops scout
through desks and drawers, scan suspect papers,
rip maps from walls, curl fists, shout

strangled threats until they left, failed raiders.
When the rain stopped, a weak sun dappled
the muddy ruts gashed by collaborators,

and the girl stepped outside to whirl, unshackled,
by herself in the rocky playground clearing.
Her face in the blanched light flushed, rattled,

but her loose hair flew in a blazing ring—
Maeve, Fianna, Dierdre of the Sorrows.
She squared her shoulders, chin up, glaring.

Her long arms were spears, her fingers, arrows.

We

At first we shared our bounty—
soothed hungry gatherers to sleep, softened
their skin, healed their wounds.
We fed them, gave them fire and soft beds.

And they gave us beautiful names—Yarrow
and Corn Flower, Burdock and Candlewick,
Lion's Tooth, and Purslane—and tended us
with careful hands, harvest hymns, water.

We watched as they began to pull
sleeping stones from meadows, to fell trees
and build barns, tame acres
of maize with scythes.

Savage when they no longer
needed us, they purged us
from gardens, tore into our homes
with their steel hoes.

But we fight back. We strangle their delicate
flowers with our bare-knuckled roots,
sprout bright, deadly berries, and leaves
oily with poisons and studded with burrs.

We spread, year after year, with abandon.
Our long veins branch deep into earth. We need
only sun or soil to grow—and wind, whispering
our beautiful names, to seed the world with our dust.

Cat and Mouse at the Broken Doll

I thought I could play the game and get by.
I thought I was as nimble as sly.
I thought I'd dance then duck and dive.

But before I could slip across the floor
I heard the click of the widening jaw
just as I felt his steely paw.

And in the ensuing frenzied waltz
all I saw was my stunned surprise
mirrored back from the brute's cold eyes.

Destroying Angels

Our fruiting bodies glisten under leaves,
growing around the roots of an old oak tree,
catching glints of moon and blossoming.
We scatter spores like gifts from ruffled gills
to consecrate and seed the forest floor.

We cast our veiled spells in the dead of night,
soothed by wind and rain, darkness and cool,
silver sisters rising from the soil,
a pixie circle—tempting and malign.

And when day breaks we lay low and listen
for hunters' heavy boots, the hungry ones,
the gangs with hanging baskets rumbling through.
We've prepared our pith and poison for the taking,
now mouth our winsome songs, and shimmer in waiting.

Martha's Letter to Jesus

I left you a tender leg
of lamb to savor to the bone,
a salty solid touch your tongue
can relish when I'm gone—

a gift to spark remembrance,
a smoky sacrifice,
the chore that quelled my voices
while I contemplated flight.

Your words last night cracked like a slap.
You stung me from the dream,
roused me to lose the demons
that chide me to cook and clean.

I grabbed Mary's shearling coat,
stole gold from Lazarus,
and slipped away before light broke
to disappear in hush.

I'm headed for a promised land,
Lord, where I'll drink and rant,
and wash men's feet with perfumed hair
and get lost in their hands.

I trust you won't be hungry
and that Mary won't be cold
while I chase your proffered miracles
down my salvation road.

Ahab's Wife

When the news of her husband's death arrived
she waited until their small son slept
to step out of her heavy clothes and plunge,
limbs gleaming, into the moonlit sea.
She swam, for one night free
and unbound, among the good and evil
creatures of the deep—the dolphins,
the sharks, the Pequod's teeming spirits—
all scattering and spinning in the wake
of the great White Whale.

Little Black Dress

Mrs. X in her little black dress, martini in hand,
smokes a cigarette, eyes Mr. Y, smoothing back
his hair, loosening his collar, rising from a chair.

She sidles by, stumbles into him, ashes on his jacket,
vodka down her chin. Mrs. X gasps, a hand against
his chest, red, lacquered nails shown off to good effect.

Mr. Y, being a gentlemanly guy, murmurs
it's no problem, and draws her outside where they slow-dance
like they did in days gone by when Mrs. X
was Mrs. Y, Coltrane flowed, and the moon hung high.

Five

❧

Honeymoon

Side-by-side on a small white towel, we bask
in the sun smeared in coconut oil. I brush
her cheek and she throws a smile. Then we go
for a swim, take a walk, go shelling.

A master collector, her bucket fills
with angel wings and glassy moon shells.
Back at the towel, she sorts through her catch,
picks out the perfect, tosses the rest.

Then we lean back, arms around our knees,
and watch the sun drop, and gulls circling,
and she tastes like salt and smells like limes
when she sits close, her head against mine.

Sweet Mary Murphy, beaming, bold,
she'll never leave me. We'll never grow old.

Water Running From the Hose

He watches her from a window,
smokes his cigarette,
sees her fumble with the nozzle,
spray the garden, soak the grass.

Stealing outside through the back door
he glides across the lawn,
puts his hands around her waist,
picks her up and spins her.

She yelps. He laughs. She throws her hat.
He kisses her neck. She kisses back.
They fall to the ground. She rolls away,
leaps to her feet, hits the spray.

Cardinals, doves—their garden's swarming.
He lays back, picks her a rose.
Seven-thirty in the morning—
water's running from the hose.

Working From Home During a Storm

We listen to ice and snow pelt the cottage
all morning between conference calls.
When we look up from our blue screens
to peer out, I look east, you north.

Finally lunchtime and together we burst
into the kitchen, ravenous—
soup and bread and,
against good judgment, wine.

I take one sip and cannot stop
and soon we're outside—me wrapped
around you on a sled, Harley-style,
flying down a crystal slope.

Later we peel off clothes
nubbed with ice and step cool-limbed
to the hearth where you build
a towering fire.

And we revel there through the long
afternoon into evening—all shadows and skin,
breath and ice, teeth and coyotes
howling for love deep in the shimmering hills.

Year-Round Beautiful

In response we build our border
year-round beautiful—tended
with coils of hand-wrigged hoses,
drenched with cool spray
every sun-struck summer morning.
Summer nights, we drink by a fire, toast
marshmallows, and the hedgerow
blossoming into border between us
and the Burleys and their tangled dump
of brush, dented bumpers, splintered
bookshelves, a cracked mirror flaring.

You chose well, husband—winterberry,
mountain laurel, and rosebays—
pink and purple splayed
across hosta-steeped black bark mulch.
And oak leaf hydrangeas billowing flowers
that white to dry rust, papery brown in fall
amidst false cypress looming
over blue maid hollies who step
from their shadows—tiny front-row dancers,
curtsying in wait for the single male's
bee-sprung exhale.

By winter, though, it's clear we haven't won.
The thriving pile of scrub, mangled
wheels, fractured grills, all mix
with our rich, organic soil to greet
the hordes of hungry rabbits and rodents,
the tall, ticky deer who step with grace
across the Burley's trash-bin haul
to rampage our songbirds' feed—

blinking and grinning as they chomp
and swill down everything crunchy,
salty, savory, leafy, or green.

Scargo Tower in December

On the roof we sit and sip spirits
while the sun drops and the sky flares
orange and pink, then dusk.
Beneath us, six flights of winding stairs
and ghosts—murmuring,
rising from the smooth inside walls.

Nauset Light Beach, November 2001

That afternoon we walked
two maybe three miles
down the deserted beach,
cold wind keeping us alert
to just-how-lucky we were.

Dark birds circled over the ocean.
The sky shifted and purpled
as we approached the dunes;
were almost on top of them
when we saw the newly-planted flag—
a testament, surely, to someone loved.

East, a distant boat rocked
black against whitecaps
and a slate gray sky.

West, the bruised sky melted
into the grasping claws of winter trees
and a light flickered
in a window
in the solitary cottage
across the marsh.

And Old Glory in the dunes
bridging ocean to marsh,
marsh to ocean,
propelling us back toward the lighthouse,
into the wind
relentlessly down
the darkening shoreline.

At Yeats's Grave

When we arrived
you licked parched lips
and hymned:
Cast a cold Eye
On Life, on Death.
Horseman, pass by.

Then we wrangled
like a couple
of highbrow scholars—
the horseman means us,
a judge, apocalypse,
eternity. The broken year
railed between us.
We circled in uncertainty,
sharpened old points
into daggers, prodded
wounds to test their borders.

Ben Bulben burned
beyond our onslaught.
Sandwort spilled
down limestone, mudstone,
shale to scree—a wheeling
free-fall until you snapped
a smashing smile
at me, astonishing
shot—flared, framed.
No ancestor from
a sepia past but the flesh
and blood my memory
had long been scrabbling after.

Getting Ready for a Grandchild's Visit

You disappear up pull-down stairs
into cluttered gloom to search
for our mothballed cache of Halloween.

I pace below, and wait for you to tender
taped up boxes, bins, bags bulging
with who knows what, imagined treasures.

Nothing's marked. For years we've stashed
away kids' report cards, trophies, dolls,
my mother's hats, your great-grand's swords.

One-by-one, you push, I pull, as our hunt-
and-retrieve job blossoms into cleanout.
We'll tackle it now while we're still able.

On our front steps I tear a carton open—
a jumble of frayed toe shoes, tutus, ribbons.
From inside the bin's dank innards, silverfish

rush and reel in cold light, dart beneath
the porch, gone before I smash them, but more
come flash dashing from a bag of magazines—

their teardrop bodies skitter, stippled pearl,
tick-tap to vanish, while we shake discarded
exoskeletons out from ancient book leaves.

Finally you find our Dollar Tree straw-strapped
scarecrows, witches, ghosts —all wrecked
but for a plastic pumpkin and one skeleton mask.

Side-by-side, on the steps, we decide we'll toss
it all except for the one bin of fairy tales
we'd sealed up tight, the pumpkin, and the skull.

Before the Blizzard

Bundled mummies, we roam
the neighborhood,
a maze of frost-heaved roads,
woods, blank-eyed homes.

The blanched air clenches,
roils for release,
leaks the hoarfrost
fragrance of dry snow.

Salt sparks silver
over cracked asphalt.
We link hands
and crisscross skeins of ice.

Above, clouds shape shift sky
into old faces—
familiar, before they split
and spill, erase us.

A Distant Mirror

You touched my hand.
Your fingers brushed a veil,
a restless finch to flight.

We left the house,
rambled buckthorn-
crowded trails,
skirted oak roots,
fallen trees until
we came upon a hut
next to a frozen swamp.

I pulled you with me
into past—Gothic
history I was sunk in—
Pest Maiden's cottage,
moss-toppled walls,
season without days
or hours. We lingered there,
braved contagion.
Ghosts of rats quavered
behind us. Coyote bayed
the wrath of Saturn.

I pointed out emerging
Venus, the crescent moon,
the sun's last glare,
drew you close, matched
your breathing. Sky refracted
in the cracked ice quag.

Gowns and Shoes and Beds of Roses

Unease steeps in our bones. It's time to go,
to flee the somnolent lull of our peeling home.
Chatham, you say, *come live with me in Chatham,*
and I agree. It seems a brilliant plan, the sea.
The strand would harbor everything we need—
summer ripe with clover, beach plum trees,
blue-green heather lolling on back dunes,
a simple cottage with a year-round view
of Monomoy's longshore zigzag drift and spit,
the rush and backwash, open ocean whip,
a place where the taste of salt might linger
on remembered skin, where tender fingers
might tremble moon shell buttons, and embered
berries blaze crimson through November.

Six

❦

To the Red Maple in Spring

March maple gathering snow outside my frost-bleared window,
you have captured my prayers in your winter branches for years.

I petition relentlessly. You sway in the pressing breeze.
Lichened bark bears remorse for lost courage, compassion.

I present my disappointments. You waver; inhale them.
God laces your ruby bulbs with pearls of spring snow.

I trust you to stream into blowsy green leafdom soon,
to stretch into star-blossom April, May, June.

I'll turn and leave you when sun razes fear to dust.
On my knees, will return, open-palmed, in due season.

Marconi Beach

Atlantic's blue heaves
white caps, churns icy foam. Spray
thrown in the air cleaves

on landing in the
swimmer's silver hair—salt drops
lit by August sun.

Head back, face to sky,
he drifts, untethered, winking
light in ocean's eye.

Beneath him teal shifts
to black. Skates skim sea's bottom.
Paired fins shiver, lift.

A sleek fish brushes
his skin—papery, thin—as
it careens through hush.

Weathered memory
sparks, thunders through limbs, surges
over reverie.

The old man turns, gropes
through surf, hollowed hands syncing
rote-remembered strokes,

back to the shore where
grandchildren crouch, stack smooth stones,
building flinty piers,

stepping stones through tide,
deep moats gashed in sandy land,
perfectly designed

for waves that fade, flow—
a sea that calls everything
it touches its own.

Alligator

I circle the same ground, suffocating
in salt. Shadows dapple the swells
that shift above my scales.

Streaming air singes my yellow eyes
when I drift up from ocean's bottom,
raise my head, blink, and gaze.

A scramble of pink, white, and brown
arms and legs, neon flowered rumps swirl
and sway to shore. Whistles wail.

I slog through the surf by instinct now,
dazzled by the silver shades of shark
that stalk in my wake.

All I desired was open
sky, open sun, a careen through water
without boundary, one clear sail,

a brief escape. Freshwater god, king
of the canal dwellers—one
wrong turn and even I topple to prey.

Providence

Off nurses' voices, emergency responses—
then finally his daughters, breathless,
rush to his side, and he promises
each time, to use the chair,
to call for help.

They never knew him
as the boy from Waldo Street
who climbed one foot, one hand
against a tree, the other against
the garage wall until he reached
the V then leapt to the roof
and from there to Casey's, then Berube's,
Mulshenock's, and Conlon's
where the adventure ends
with the long jump down.

Father

The old man rules his kingdom from a chair.
He wields his power through a glare.

With a tap of the remote always by his side
he commandeers the TV guide.

His phone, placed strategically past arm's length,
requires him to stretch to build his strength.

He fumes when his shaky legs give way
and vows he'll walk again one day.

His doctors claim it's not possible
but he knows he's unstoppable.

In firm command of each and every breath
he steels his will to outwit death.

Brightview on Blueberry Hill

Thighs thwapping beneath her multi-colored mu-mu,
Flo barrels into the dining room behind her walker,
commandeers her place—the purple satin chair—
at the head of the popular ladies' table.

Even the deaf diners can hear her piercing demands,
her piped pronouncements regarding the food, the servers,
the ladies themselves, and their exquisite Monday
morning manicures, their white, coiffed hair.

She buzzes with intensity, rustles her ass back
and forth across the seat to smooth her rumpled
underwear. She guzzles her Royal yellow Jell-O
with the gusto of a nubile teen, eyeing the new

men wheeling in. She snaps out verdicts—one to ten—
while the ladies nod and wipe their specs to get
an unobstructed view since the men are so few and far
between on this lolling blue hill in the kingdom of Flo.

An Old Man Sings

A woman plays songs from the forties on
a piano so grand it takes up a third of the room.
In the front row, from his wheelchair,
an old man croons the lyrics in a whispery tenor.

For the first time in eighty-four years,
since Miss Allen made him mouth the words
in the first grade concert, he is a welcome
member of the chorus—and he cannot contain
the young boy's jubilant, toothless grin.

An Old Man in His Chair

The sea churns. Boats skirt the rocks
in the painting he hung in his little den years ago.
Now, he rides the waves as he files his nails.
Sometimes his children, smiling out
from another frame, join him. Though most days
he conjures their voices and recites, in order,
the beautiful names he gave them.
Then he stretches out in his chair on the smooth
back of a boulder, and lets the sea rush through him.

Late Love

They meet in the green
foyer of the old age home.
Delia's eyes bob behind glasses
balanced just-so on her nose.
She glints through smudges.

It's Jim's first day.
His daughter's late, and it's dull here
in the dripping north, and dark,
so far from Carolina and his boat
and Bang, his dog now living
with a friend in Raleigh.

Delia asks the questions.
He murmurs, smiles, molasses eyes,
from his carbon fiber chair—
a vehicle of modern sort,
equipped with a smart right arm lever.

She grasps the handles, navigates it
down the hall, through a door,
and to a table where
some old folks sip sloe gin
and Lena Horne sings *Stormy Weather.*

Sundown

I cradle the ivory pendant between my palms
while behind me shadows climb, flicker and spin,
and when I press it softly, squarely in the middle,
an angel slips in through my moon-washed window.

She glows in her nurse's white, her soft words soothing,
as she settles the alabaster charm with quiet hands,
and we stare into the dark courtyard together—
hair pale, eyes milky, though it's not because I'm old.

It's a trick of light, a match, a flare that falters
after twilight when all color seeps and alters.

The Blue Chair Laments

Jack Mullen left
alone against
the posted rules
he could not read
despite their bold
dark lettering and glasses
pressed onto his nose
he pushed himself
from contoured space
from cushions concave
with his weight
he set out on
his own two feet
in full belief
across the water
ridged mountains rose
tipped streaming sky
lost king's thin crown
and sweeping gyre
of grey osprey
the knife-edged flash
the salt-stung prey
still Jack moved out
at steady pace
into the sun's
sea-blinding light
not a Peter
more a Paul
he turned and beckoned
before he fell

In a Cedar-Scented Drawer

Long after the long
winter, after the life
saving knife and the raw
boned surgeon's deft
handiwork, she left
behind shivers
of silky slips amidst old
lady underwear, sachets
of silvery scent, and a cool
cloth breast. Its lace-
trimmed lip opened
in my hand like a French
Angel fish, billowed four
round satin-kissed pillows,
slip-synced in sequence
for years to simulate
her size B-30
beneath her summer
sheaths, her winter
blues, a cocoon of bosom
buddies to fill the yawning
Bosom Buddy, who'd required
so little, only, according
to its faded tag, to be hand
washed warm and laid
on a towel to dry.

Winter at a Summer House

The walls shrink close,
the pipes heave a last shudder,
and snow seals the hush.
Ghosts huddle under blankets,
shivering through long nights
to the *tap, tap, tap*
of a loose shutter.

When a floorboard groans
at an unexpected touch
of light, they fling off
their covers and roam
the house, waking up others
dozing under eaves,
in closets.

They slip outside to the jetty
where one of them hovers
on the point, then dives,
and they cheer, their silvery
cries soaring as she rises
and plummets on the swells
of the white winter sea.

About the Author

Mary Beth Hines grew up in Massachusetts, where she spent Saturday afternoons ditching ballet to pursue stories and poems deep in the stacks of the Waltham Public Library. She earned a bachelor of arts in English from The College of the Holy Cross and studied for a year at Durham University in England. She began a regular creative writing practice following a career in public service (Volpe Center, Cambridge, Massachusetts), leading award-winning national outreach, communications, and workforce programs. Her poetry, short fiction, and non-fiction appear in dozens of literary journals and anthologies nationally and abroad. *Winter at a Summer House* is her first poetry collection. When not reading or writing, she swims, walks in the woods, plays with friends, travels with her husband, and enjoys life with their family, including their two beloved grandchildren, Travis and Julia.

Visit her online at
www.marybethhines.com.

Made in the USA
Middletown, DE
21 December 2021

54624784R00061